Exploring Money

Saving Money

by Connor Stratton

FOCUS READERS®

PIONEER

www.focusreaders.com

Focus Readers is distributed by North Star Editions: sales@northstareditions.com | 888-417-0195

Produced for Focus Readers by Red Line Editorial.

Photographs ©: Shutterstock Images, cover, 1, 4, 6, 8, 10, 12, 14, 16–17, 18, 21

Library of Congress Cataloging-in-Publication Data
Names: Stratton, Connor, author.
Title: Saving money / by Connor Stratton.
Description: Lake Elmo, MN : Focus Readers, [2023] | Series: Exploring money | Includes index. | Audience: Grades 2-3
Identifiers: LCCN 2022012292 (print) | LCCN 2022012293 (ebook) | ISBN 9781637392409 (hardcover) | ISBN 9781637392928 (paperback) | ISBN 9781637393956 (pdf) | ISBN 9781637393444 (ebook)
Subjects: LCSH: Finance, Personal--Juvenile literature. | Money--Juvenile literature. | Saving and investment--Juvenile literature.
Classification: LCC HG179 .S84517 2023 (print) | LCC HG179 (ebook) | DDC 332.024--dc23/eng/20220311
LC record available at https://lccn.loc.gov/2022012292
LC ebook record available at https://lccn.loc.gov/2022012293

Printed in the United States of America
Mankato, MN
082022

About the Author

Connor Stratton writes and edits nonfiction children's books. Growing up, he helped his dad collect the 50 State Quarters.

Table of Contents

Chapter 1

Saving Goals

People **spend** money on many things. Some items are cheap. But other things are costly. So, people often **save** their money.

People earn money at jobs. But people don't spend all their money right away. Instead, they keep some money for later. Over time, their savings grow. Then, they use their savings to pay for costly items.

Did You Know?

Many people use **budgets**. That helps them know how much they should save.

Chapter 2

Meeting Needs

Savings help people meet their needs. Suppose a man makes $2,000 a month. He uses $1,000 to pay his **rent**. Then he spends $800 on bills. He has $200 left in savings.

The next month, the man makes $2,000 again. But his car breaks down. It will cost $400 to fix. The man still has to pay $1,000 for his rent. He still has to spend $800 on his bills. That leaves him with $200 for the month. He also has $200 saved from last month. So, he can use his savings to fix his car.

Chapter 3

Banks

People often put their savings in banks. Banks make sure the money stays safe. Banks also keep track of the money. They use **bank accounts**.

In some bank accounts, money can be taken out right away. In others, it must stay for a long time. But banks help the money grow. Over time, people can get more than they put in.

Did You Know? Many people save money for **retirement.** That way, they have enough money in old age.

Interest

Many bank accounts have **interest**.
The money grows a little each year.
Suppose a girl puts $100 in a bank.
The interest is 1 percent. Her money
grows by 1 percent each year.

2023

One percent of $100 is $1. So, after one year, the girl earns $1. Now she has $101.

2024   2025

Chapter 4

Saving Up

Suppose a boy wants a new hat. The hat costs $10. He earns $2 every day for his chores. He decides to save up.

Each day, the boy saves the $2 from his chores. After five days, he has $10 in savings. Now he can **afford** the new hat!

FOCUS ON
Saving Money

Write your answers on a separate piece of paper.

1. Write a sentence that explains the main idea of Chapter 2.

2. Do you think it's better to keep your savings in a bank or at home? Why?

3. What do savings help people pay for?
- **A.** cheap items
- **B.** bank accounts
- **C.** costly items

4. Suppose you want a new pair of shoes that cost $50. You have $30 in savings. How much more money do you need to save to buy the shoes?
- **A.** $10
- **B.** $20
- **C.** $50

Answer key on page 24.

Glossary

afford
To have enough money to pay for something.

bank accounts
Places where people put their money to keep it safe.

budgets
Tools that help people keep track of how much they save and spend.

interest
An extra amount of money that a bank gives to people who keep their money in the bank.

rent
Money a person pays to live in a house or apartment.

retirement
When people are no longer working, often in old age.

save
To set money aside so it can be used later.

spend
To use money to pay for something.

To Learn More

BOOKS

Gaertner, Meg. *Spending and Saving Money.*
Minneapolis: Abdo Publishing, 2018.

Huddleston, Emma. *Managing Money.* Lake Elmo, MN:
Focus Readers, 2021.

NOTE TO EDUCATORS

Visit **www.focusreaders.com** to find lesson plans,
activities, links, and other resources related to this title.

Index

Answer Key: **1.** Answers will vary; **2.** Answers will vary; **3.** C; **4.** B